A publication of CCM Creative Ventures / Writer: Shari MacDonald / Art Direction & Design: Mike Rapp, Gear/Nashville / Cover & Back Photographs: Kerri McKeehan-Stuart / Interior Photographs: Kerri McKeehan-Stuart and Various

Audio Adrenaline contact information—Internet: www.audioa.com / Management: BrickHouse Entertainment, P.O. Box 681765, Franklin, TN 37068-1765 615/771-1180 / Booking: William Morris Agency, 2100 West End Avenue #1000, Nashville, TN 37203 615/963-3000

Audio Adrenaline is ... all smiles? Clockwise, from top, Ben Cissell, Bob Herdman, Mark Stuart, Barry Blair and Will McGinniss.

IT'S BEEN NEARLY A DECADE since the original members of Audio Adrenaline first felt the rush that comes from mixing a love for rock music with a passion for ministry. But don't look for the group to crash anytime soon. The buzz surrounding

Audio A has been building steadily since the early nineties, yet the boys today are soaring higher than ever—and there's no end to their flight in sight.

With fifteen number one radio hits, three Dove Awards, one Billboard Music Award nomination, and three Grammy nominations to their credit, Audio Adrenaline has become one of the most respected and loved bands in Christian

Some kind of zombies: Cissell, Herdman, Stuart and McGinniss.

music. More than that, its members have played a key role in shaping the sound of contemporary Christian rock, all while maintaining the humility—and the playful spirit—of the boys next door. Not bad for a band that started as a fluke and was never supposed to see the light of day—much less touch hearts and impact lives around the world.

THE BIRTH OF A BRAND

(Just not the band you think)

The boys in the band: Clockwise, from top, Mark, Bob, Will, Barry and Ben.

THE FIRST DAYS OF COLLEGE mark the beginning of a new phase in any student's life. For Mark Stuart, Audio Adrenaline's husky-voiced lead vocalist, and Barry Blair, the band's original guitarist, Kentucky Christian

College (KCC) would do more than stretch their minds and broaden their horizons. It would provide a testing ground for a ministry that would ultimately touch millions of souls.

Barry expressed his desire to start a band soon after the two met at school. That dream was quickly realized as they began to piece together the group that would be Audio Adrenaline's musical predecessor: A-180. Fellow KCC student Will McGinniss was their next recruit.

"I met Will my freshman year," recalls Mark. "His mom actually introduced him to me. This was the first week of school, and she was hanging out at a hotel, making sure everything was okay." Somehow, Will's mother found out what Mark and Barry were planning. "She said, 'I heard you're starting a band. My son plays bass guitar. You need to get him in your band.'"

That sounded good to Mark and Barry. There was only one hitch: Will had received his bass as a high school graduation present. "He had only been playing for a couple of months," Mark remembers, "so he was fresh off the vine."

"It was crazy," agrees Will (who is also known as "Bill" to the guys in the band). But apparently the two more experienced musicians saw potential in the budding bassist because they announced: "Yeah, you're cool. We'll just teach ya."

"Barry had been playing for a long time and was a killer guitar player, even at 18 years old," says Mark. "Killer chops. He could do anything. He taught Bill how to play bass and that's how we started as A-180: with my brother, David Stuart (keyboards and background vocals); myself; Barry Blair; Will McGinniss; and Ron Gibson (drummer)."

A-180 quickly made a name for itself locally as an old-school Christian rock band with a mission to tell audiences about God. They accomplished their goal by performing what Mark calls "rootsy, rock-album kind of stuff," covering groups like The Altar Boys, Russ Taff, and U2. Ultimately, the band's popularity was so great, the school was booking them nearly every weekend. The group recorded two albums while at KCC.

During their college years, Mark, Will, and Barry also made friends with a zany fellow student named Bob Herdman—a former Airborne Ranger who'd spent his

army career jumping out

of planes and calling in

airstrikes—who was

attending Kentucky

Christian on a GI bill.

"Bob had this real

flair about him," remem-

bers Mark. "A kind of

*Christian music's "Underdogs": Tyler
Burkum, Mark Stuart, Ben Cissell, Bob
Herdman and Will McGinniss*

THE BLUE TRUCK

"Our first van was used as a dog house before we bought it," remembers Mark. "We wrecked that van about two months later in Illinois because it didn't have any brakes, and we were pulling a 10,000 lb. trailer. And I happened to be driving at the time, which was cool because I still can't drive in the state of Illinois."

After this incident, the guys developed a special relationship with their second van, a Ryder vehicle dubbed "The Blue Truck," which they converted into a bus.

"We made it bigger three times because we kept needing less storage space and more room for people to sleep," remembers Will.

Mark adds: "She was a work-in-progress, for sure. We almost died in this truck. We had carbon monoxide poisoning from riding in the back at Atlanta Fest. We woke up and everybody had these big-time headaches and could hardly even walk. We had to have two ambulances come out and we were on oxygen for a couple of hours each, trying to get over this carbon monoxide poisoning. So that's when we changed the truck a little bit."

NOTE: Audio Adrenaline later rented the Blue Truck to Hokus Pick for a tour, then sold it to the Supertones—who blew up the engine and in turn sold it to the Insyderz. Rumor has it that the Blue Truck is still in existence—possibly in the possession of Project 86. For a glimpse of the inside of the Blue Truck, take a peek at Audio Adrenaline's "Big House" long form video.

abandon and life. I really kind of picked up on his personality and fell in love with him as a friend. We would ride around in his Jeep, and he started running sound for us in A-180. He was a terrible sound guy. All he would do is sit around and talk to girls and stuff, and the sound would be feeding back....That's how he started getting kind of interested in music and wanted to be involved in what we were doing."

While this was the beginning of Bob's involvement with A-180, it was far from the end. For, despite Bob's lack of musical background, God would use this onetime army ranger to shake up this popular local group and lead it into a ministry far greater than anything they could have hoped for or planned.

It's hard to resist the infectious energy of an Audio A show.

BOB HERDMAN DIDN'T SING. Bob Herdman didn't play an instrument. But that didn't stop Bob Herdman from wanting to be part of a band.

"I came up with the name probably a year before [Audio Adrenaline was formed], just goofing around in a dorm room with a bunch of guys," he says. While listening to loud music and jumping around, playing air guitar, Bob thought to himself: *This is like audio adrenaline; it gets you all pumped up!*

The phrase stuck in his head. Not long thereafter, Bob says, "I heard this song—I think it was by Anthrax, called 'I'm the Man.' It was like a heavy metal rap song. And I thought, Man, wouldn't it be so cool if there was Christian music that sounded like this?"

The seeds of this idea germinated as he traveled with his buddies in A-180, running sound and helping to load and unload equipment. Then one day, Bob—who had dabbled in poetry writing throughout college and had already written the lyrics for the A-180 tune "DC-10"—scratched out the words to a crazy, little offbeat song he called

"My God."

Buddha was a fat man / So what? / Mohammed thought he had a plan / I guess not. / A Hindu god is an old cow / You could be a god if you knew how…

> "I heard this song—I think it was by Anthrax, called 'I'm the Man.' It was like a heavy metal rap song. And I thought, Man, wouldn't it be so cool if there was Christian music that sounded like this?"

"I thought, This is kinda cool; it's kinda weird," says Bob. "So I talked Mark and Barry into going into a studio. I said I would pay for it if they would write heavy metal rap music. They had only been in the studio a couple times and were like, 'Oh, yeah. Anything to go into the studio again! Even if this is dumb: if someone's gonna pay for it, we'll go!'

"So we worked on it, and Barry wrote all these cool guitar licks—and Mark and I both sang. I didn't know how to sing. I wasn't going to, but we thought it would be cool if someone acted like they were rapping—you know a real harsh voice—but I couldn't even stay on beat. Mark would have to tap me hard on the shoulder when it was time to say my words!"

Since the recording was not, in the strictest sense, an A-180 endeavor, the

The Audio A guys, holding auditions for back-up vocalists.

guys decided to give their spin-off group its own name. And so—presumably for one song only—Audio Adrenaline was born.

After paying for the "My God" recording with funds from his savings and his army college fund, Bob had a little bit of money left over to use in promoting the song.

"I heard about this lady, Nancy Reese, who had a compilation CD that went out to different radio stations. So we paid, I think, $800 to get it put on this CD. She sent it out, and there were only maybe ten Christian stations in the whole country that played any kind of Christian heavy metal/rap at the time."

The unique musical style and unusual lyrics stood out among the selections, making a strong impression on DJs around the country.

"It got some attention because it was so weird," reasons Bob.

Their promoter was also responsible for tracking the song to see how often it was played. Bob Herdman got into the act as well, phoning radio stations from his dorm and asking, "Hey, are you playing 'My God'? You should play this 'My God' song and let people hear it."

"After that," says Mark, "it started snowballing and people started requesting it. Even in Australia, Europe…everywhere, it was taking off. It was really bizarre. We were just going, 'What in the world is going on? This is weird.'"

Before long, "My God" had reached number five on the hard rock charts. It had also caught the attention of ForeFront Records president Dan Brock.

Brock called the band and offered them a record deal based on that one song.

The group's response was not what you might expect.

"We actually turned him down," says Bob, "because this was just a band we made up. We didn't really have any [more] songs."

"ForeFront offered the record deal to Audio Adrenaline, which wasn't really a band at the time," says Mark. "It was a joke really, something we were doing for fun."

"ForeFront offered the record deal to Audio Adrenaline, which wasn't really a band at the time," says Mark. "It was a joke really, something we were doing for fun."

About three months later, however, with the offer still on the table, the group decided that ministering as Audio Adrenaline was perhaps what God was calling them to do.

Mark recalls: "The members of the other band, A-180, said, 'Well, why don't you guys become Audio Adrenaline? Bob becomes part of the band, and you do this crazy style of music.'"

> "[The new Audio Adrenaline CD] might not have been the greatest thing, musically, in the world. But it was definitely something fresh, bold, and exciting."

Mark, Will, and Barry agreed to transition into Audio Adrenaline. For a short time, Mark's brother David was in Audio Adrenaline as well, though he soon left in order to focus on his new family.

With the new group came both new challenges and new opportunities.

"It kind of shook it up and changed it around a bit, which was totally God," says Mark. "In the beginning," he claims, "it might not have been the greatest thing, musically, in the world. But it was definitely something fresh, bold, and exciting."

Fresh, bold, and exciting was precisely what their label, ForeFront Records, was looking for. But in order for such a ministry to take shape, the group needed more than a new name. They needed new songs. They needed a new album.

And so Audio Adrenaline went to Nashville—where ForeFront was located—to begin their new career. "There," says Bob, "we started from scratch. We just wrote some funny songs, and kind of had to go to work."

Uh, Barry, the camera's this way: (l-r) McGinniss, Stuart, Herdman, Cissell and Blair.

IN NASHVILLE, THE MEM-BERS OF AUDIO ADRENALINE DIDN'T JUST HAVE TO WORK ON THEIR SONGS. They had to work at "real jobs" simply to survive.

27

"There were four of us at that time: Barry, Bob, me, and Will," says Mark, "and we all lived in a two-bedroom apartment. Bob at that point wasn't living off his GI bill anymore. His aunt passed away [and left him some money]. So the rest of us got jobs while Bob wrote poetry for another year! I worked at the Cracker Barrel, and I met a lot of famous country music people there. Will was appraising houses and Barry worked at the Ponderosa as a

Billy Graham takes a "Free Ride" with the members of Audio A

busboy. We did that while we were making our album. We were really poor. Those of us who were brave enough donated plasma—that was me and Will, basically. I still have a scar today."

On a practical level, the guys were simply trying to survive. But finding their identity as a new band was an even greater challenge.

"When we first started, ForeFront wanted us to be this kind of out-there, weird, over-the-top [group] lyrically: a hybrid of rap and metal music—which was very cool," says Mark, "but we were kind of young at the time and we didn't really know what we were doing. So the first record is like a hodgepodge of a lot of different sounds," including hip-hop and rock. Not only that, "We had done 'My God' as a joke, so we were kind of in a predicament because we didn't really know how to do this. We had to rewrite a lot of songs for the first record."

Despite the difficulty of the challenge, Mark says, the process was a blessing. "A lot of times we blame our label for this weird beginning, but they kind of pushed us to do something different—something a little out of the ordinary. It was cool that it worked out like that."

The group's next big break came when they were chosen to tour with Geoff Moore and The Distance.

"It was hard work, to say the least," remembers Mark. "We were the crew and the drivers on that tour as well as the opening band. Bob and I would drive all night. We drove the bus, which really wasn't a bus—it was a minibus, like a church would have. Barry and Will would set up sound and lights all day and we would all tear down at the end of the night and take off for the next show."

Despite all the hard work, success was not immediate.

"We were going to get dropped after our first album from ForeFront Records because the album didn't really do as

Mark Stuart accepts the first Gold Record for Audio A, 1996's Bloom.

well as they planned," Mark remembers. "They spent a lot of money and we did an expensive video, but it just didn't blow up like they wanted it to."

Rumor has it that dcTalk's Toby McKeehan went to bat for the group, arguing: "You've got to keep Audio Adrenaline around for one more record and see what they can do."

The label decided to give the band another chance, and it wasn't until two or three albums—long after the crisis was over—that the guys from Audio A learned of the near-miss.

Fortunately, their next album, *Don't Censor Me*, provided the hit ForeFront had been looking for.

"With *Don't Censor Me*, we felt a lot more in control of the songwriting," says Mark. "It's almost like ForeFront was bored with us at this time and they were [saying], 'Just come make a record and we'll see what happens.' We got some reins of control back and it was a step towards us becoming ourselves again. 'Big House' came out of that one. We started working with the Gotee Brothers: Todd Collins and Joey Elwood. Then we went on the spring 1994 *Free At Last* tour with dcTalk, and that record was the record that started to really take off. Our label started to freak out. They started getting a lot of sales, and they were really excited again.

"'My God' got us a record deal, but 'Big House' was the beginning of our career."

BY THE TIME AUDIO ADRENALINE'S THIRD

ALBUM, *Bloom*, released in February

1996, the band's success

was firmly established.

Evidence of their over-

whelming popularity

More coffee please: Audio Adrenaline in the early days, getting ready to hit the road again.

included one Dove Award (1996 Best Long Form Video, "Big House"); coverage in *Rolling Stone* magazine; performances at the Hard Rock Cafe and the legendary House of Blues; numerous Billboard Music Award and ACMA Award nominations; and new tours with the Newsboys (*Going Public*, spring 1995) and dcTalk (*Jesus Freak*, spring 1996). A tour with Steven Curtis Chapman (*Signs of Life*, fall 1996/spring 1997) and a book

> "With *Bloom*, we wanted to make a record that was classic—that if you heard it ten years from now, you really couldn't tell where it came from in the timeline of music."

about the experiences of seven students who joined them for a week of that tour (*Some Kind of Journey*, Standard Publishing) would soon follow.

"With *Bloom*, we wanted to make a record that was classic—that if you heard it ten years from now, you really couldn't tell where it came from in the timeline of music," says Mark. "There wasn't a song as big as 'Big House,' but there were a lot of songs that really touched a lot of people—songs that were fan favorites."

Unlike *Audio Adrenaline* and *Don't Censor Me*, *Bloom* was not geared to any one demographic. Rock and roll fans, adult fans, younger fans, and radio station DJs all embraced the album. "Everybody liked that record," Mark theorizes, "because it was just real simple. We were starting to gain a lot of adult fans because of the classic sound of *Bloom*. But also we were able to get in front of a lot of kids on the dcTalk tour. So it was a good time for us."

It was also a time of tremendous change. Within the previous two years, all four of the band's members had kissed bachelorhood goodbye.

"There was one point when Barry, Bob, and myself realized that we had the month of December off," says Will, "and we had been dating our girlfriends for quite some time. We were like, 'We want to get married.' Literally, there

Gentlemen, start your engine: The Audio A guys proudly display their entry at the Nashville Motor Speedway.

was one month to do it in. So we all three just went and got hitched, and then we got right out on tour again."

One year later Mark followed suit.

Achieving a balance between a touring ministry and family life proved to be possible, but difficult. The majority of the band members eventually made the adjustment, but after *Bloom*, virtuoso guitarist Barry Blair decided that life on the road was no longer for him.

"It was at that point where people kind of dug in," says Will. "In Barry's case, he felt that it wasn't something that he wanted to do as a newly married person, based on his structure. He wanted to be more of a homebody. For Bob and Mark and me, it really did blend well with our home situations. Our wives were very independent and very supportive of our ministry and wanted us to continue to do it, so they gave us their blessing. Of course, they're number one in our lives. If we didn't have their blessing, we wouldn't be doing this at all."

Mark, Will, and Bob continued to move forward. But Barry's departure left a gaping hole—one that impacted them greatly as they prepared for their fourth album, the experimental *Some Kind of Zombie*.

"A lot of people think it's a real dark record," Mark says of *Zombie*. "The title itself is kind of scary. But it's really a record about transition. It's about being changed. Being transformed from death into life. The whole concept behind it was this real mystifying kind of trippy Christian transformation.

"I think *Zombie* was a record for us to be kind of self-indulgent in a way—just kind of goof around in the studio and not really worry [about] whether people are going to get it or not, but just make a record that we really liked."

Still, the songs did not come easily.

"Basically, Will, Bob, and I were writing songs for the album,"

While having fun is optimal, the members of Audio A take their concerts and their mission very seriously.

reflects Mark. "[Prior to that], Barry was our main musical writer. He provided a lot of musical hooks to the music. So *Zombie* was a record where we didn't have Barry to lean on."

As a result, he admits, *Zombie* included both hit songs (such as the 1999 Dove Award winner for Best Rock Song, "Some Kind of Zombie") and sleepers.

"But it's an album that I really like. I'm very proud of that record, specifically for a few songs I think are really cool.

*Never fear—*Underdog *is here—the 1999 release from Audio Adrenaline featuring the concert favorite "Get Down."*

That was a changing time for us and a transitional period."

Some Kind of Zombie marked not just the last Audio Adrenaline recording by Barry Blair (on "Some Kind of Zombie"), but also the debut of two new band members: drummer Ben Cissell and guitarist Tyler Burkum.

By that time, Ben was a full-fledged member of Audio Adrenaline. Tyler had just appeared on the scene.

"Tyler wasn't even in the band officially," says Mark. "He was still trying out. We had a three-month time period where he was trying out in the summer on kind of a trial period. But we liked his guitar playing so much we wanted him to play on the record."

In fact, they liked the 17-year-old's playing so well, they soon asked him to stay permanently.

Some Kind of Zombie provided Audio Adrenaline's new bandmates an opportunity to work together for the very first time. Fans enjoyed the results of those efforts on Audio A's 1998 *Zombie* tour and 1999 Tour. The band's next album, *Underdog*, and its sup-

> "We produced the majority of [Underdog] ourselves. We really wanted the record to end up how it sounded in our heads."

porting fall 1999/spring 2000 tour gave the guys the chance to show what they could do once their considerable talents had been given some time to mix and gel.

"For *Underdog*, we had all been together as a group for years," says Mark. "Tyler had been with us about three years and Ben about five. We were all writing *Underdog* together. Tyler was writing songs. Ben was helping write songs. We produced the majority of this record ourselves," he says, along with the help of industry heavy-hitters Charlie Peacock and Todd Collins. "We really wanted the record to end up how it sounded in our heads."

"But the main priority," suggests Tyler, "was having fun."

Featuring songs like "Underdog," "Mighty Good Leader," and "Get Down" (winner of the 2000 Dove Award for Best Rock Song), the album did indeed turn out to be fun, brilliant, and exciting—just like the guys who made it.

High energy turns introspective as Mark Stuart shares his heart onstage.

MARK STUART IS ARGUABLY ONE OF THE MOST

TALENTED and likeable front men in

Christian music. But in his heart of

hearts, he is simply: "The Kid."

Guitarist Tyler Burkum remembers,

"When he started getting around 30,

AUDIO Q&A:

Q: What's the band's favorite on-tour hobby?
A: Snowboarding. The guys also play a lot of basketball on the road to keep them sane.

Q: What pets do Mark and Kerri own?
A: Mark and his bride are the loving owners of two German short-hair pointers. "One's name is Vegas, after where we got married," says Mark. The other is named Vienna, after the city where Kerri was born.

Q: What career field did three Audio Adrenaline members plan to enter prior to the success of their band?
A: Education. Mark and Bob studied secondary education at Kentucky Christian College; Will, elementary ed.

Q: Do you have a most embarrassing moment that you can share?
A: "I do, but I can't share it. It's way too gross."
—Mark Stuart

Mark made this big thing that he was really gonna work out and get back in shape. It wasn't really a midlife crisis; it was just an excuse to set a goal that he probably had always wanted to set. Right when I joined the band he was in the middle of doing it, and he always refers to himself as 'The Kid,' like a joke. Like: 'Don't mess with The Kid.'

"So we went cliff diving in

Kentucky, probably the second week I was in the band. This is a place that Bill and Mark are all like, 'Oh, yeah. We jumped off here all the time. We'll show you!' And me and [drummer] Ben [Cissell] go up to the cliff and we just jump off—it was really, really high, about 45 feet—and then Bill jumped a couple

When I said I wanted to be in a band, this isn't exactly what I meant: Mark, decked out in his finest early band attire.

of times. They were saying how they were going to school us. Mark's a lot older than I am, but he schools me. He's probably more in his prime than I am, you know?

"And he's talking about how he's gonna jump off this cliff and how he's gonna show us...but he hasn't jumped off. So we're like, 'Okay. Come on. Jump!' And he

Are you ready to rock? Stuart exhibits his enthusiasm and passion onstage.

jumps, and all these kids are watching, and he just goes into the water—*bloop*—as stiff as a board... And we were like: *Where is he?* Then we hear him yell from up the river: 'THE KID'S STILL GOT IT!'

"For the next three months his back was messed up from that one cliff dive."

Born in Kentucky, "The Kid" spent his childhood in the small town of Owensboro. Up until the time Mark entered the third grade, his father worked as a high school teacher. Then Drex Stuart entered the pastorate, serving as a preacher and then later—along with his wife and daughter—as a missionary to Haiti.

During those early years, Mark learned a lot about ministry work and leadership from watching his father.

"Being a pastor's kid, there's a lot of extra pressure and you get to learn real fast about how the church really works: the downfalls and the upsides. But you also grow up really fast as a Christian because you see a lot of what the pastor goes through during the week. That's [both] kind of cool and not-so-cool.

"But I had a great childhood. I love my parents. My older brother is [the one] who really encouraged me to become a musician in the first place. We sang all of our lives growing up; we would sing little songs where we would do harmony together. I started playing drums in sixth grade and he played keyboards, so we started getting bands together." David was also the one who later encouraged Mark to start singing in bands.

"I didn't really know that Christian groups existed until I was in high school and

ONE ON ONE

"Mark is the very analytical, very politically correct guy. The most stable, if you will. He doesn't stay mad long and it's hard for him to get mad. He's going to be an awesome producer some day. He's incredible now, and I think he can be world-class later in life. Really, he can do anything he wants." —Will McGinniss

"Mark's the kind of guy that, even when he doesn't have a clue to what's going on, he can kind of convince everybody that he does. He's a really cool leader." —Tyler Burkum

"Mark is probably the most stable person I've ever met in my life. He never loses his temper. He's probably the one I talk to the most and will just tell it to me straight. I respect him spiritually the most.

"For practical jokes, I hide his stuff a lot. [Also], he was the first one to get hit with the sink thing. I fixed [the sink on the tour bus] so the top comes off. The little goose neck that comes down would just come off—you can just unscrew it—so as soon as you turn it on the thing would just pop off and spray right at you.

"I left the room for just a second and he came in to brush his teeth. He had just woken up and the sink came off and sprayed on him. He thought that he broke it. So he was standing there still, getting wet, trying to stop it." —Ben Cissell

my brother brought home a tape from a retreat at Kentucky Christian. It was Michael W. Smith—who I'd never heard of—and DeGarmo and Key. The next year he brought home a White Heart tape. So I started really listening to this music and thinking, This is

It's either Mark Stuart just getting out of bed, or perhaps an early theatrical appearance he doesn't want us to see. Or maybe it's both.

really good. I like it. It's cool. I was challenged and uplifted by it at the same time. I was just listening to secular music before that and getting influenced, bandwise, from that."

Musically, Mark learned from such groups as Van Halen, Foreigner, Def

> "I didn't really know that Christian groups existed until I was in high school and my brother brought home a tape from a retreat at Kentucky Christian. It was Michael W. Smith—who I'd never heard of—and DeGarmo and Key."

Leppard, Duran Duran, and Bryan Adams. But he was also impacted musically—and, more importantly, spiritually—by his father, who was an accomplished musician in his own right.

Today, Mark continues to grow musically: as a singer, songwriter, front man, and producer (he produced Jennifer Knapp's *Kansas* and *Lay It Down*). But even more important to him is his growth as a man of God and as a husband.

Married to Kerri McKeehan Stuart—sister of dcTalk's Toby McKeehan—

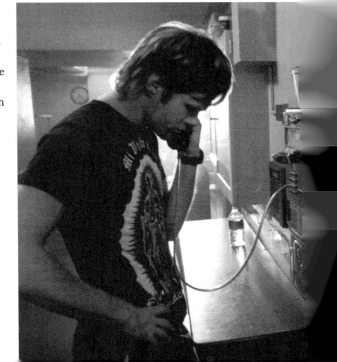

M.S. phone home: Before the show, Mark takes a moment to chat with wife Kerri.

for more than five years (the two eloped on New Year's Day), Mark still gushes like a newlywed about his bride.

"It's a goofy line from *Jerry McGuire*," he says, "but my wife definitely 'completes me.' I'm kind of stupid and goofy, but she's the coolest person I ever met. I was really taken by her sense of fun and all that. When we get together, it's like a hand and glove.

"My goal in my marriage is, I want to get to know her better and better every day. She's a well—and I need to tap into that well and experience more of that water."

Audio A bassist Will McGinniss at home with son Satchel.

RAISED AMONG THE CORN FIELDS OF

OHIO in a small farming town, Will

McGinniss and his two siblings—

twin Kimberly and younger sister,

Sonia—grew up in an idyllic setting

under less than ideal circumstances.

AUDIO Q&A:

Q: Will, when is your birthday?
A: "February 25th."
Q: The year?
A: "I've forgotten that part."

Q: Is it "Will" or "Bill"?
A: "For those of us who've know him forever, it's 'Bill.' He changed his name to Will, his stage name, about ten years ago. I can't get used to calling him Will. So he's 'Bill' to me." —Mark Stuart

Q: What is your ideal career for your son?
A: "I've been praying for my son to be the next Billy Graham. It would be so cool. He has such a godly countenance that people just see that and respect it."

Will's Pets
Will's family includes a loving wife, Andrea (who is expecting their second child), and an adorable son, Satchel, along with two pets: Siberian huskies Jake and Kioka.

"I came from a broken family," says Will. "My mom was married and divorced three times and ended up raising us three kids by herself. So, needless to say, all that kind of left me really insecure: an unloved, really weird person.

"In high school, I was a product of the original alternative scene: very early U2, New Order, Violent

Femmes—what was called 'alternative' back then. That was my freshman year. I was an outcast and a loner, kind of a weirdo person, so it kind of fit."

But Will would not remain an outcast.

"I got into a church my sophomore year of high school, and that's when I became a

"Jesus has helped me with my relationships with people and my family and, in general, cleaned me up a whole lot."

Christian. Finally, when I met Jesus, that's when the healing really started to happen. But it didn't happen right away. I was still kind of messed up for several years after. I'm still dealing with a lot of that today, but I have a greater grasp on it. Jesus has helped me with my relationships with people and my family and, in general, cleaned me up a whole lot."

Not only did Will find healing, he found himself called into ministry as he and the members of A-180 shared the gospel of Christ locally, through music.

"Barry [Blair] was very instrumental in teaching me. Then I just started learning all my favorite songs—all the early alternative music I loved to listen to. That's probably what shaped my style." Will also learned from listening to groups that played at Kentucky Christian. "A lot of the old greats came through our campus, like DeGarmo and Key, WhiteHeart, Glad, Geoff Moore &

You know, it really hurts when I do this: Audio Adrenaline's McGinniss.

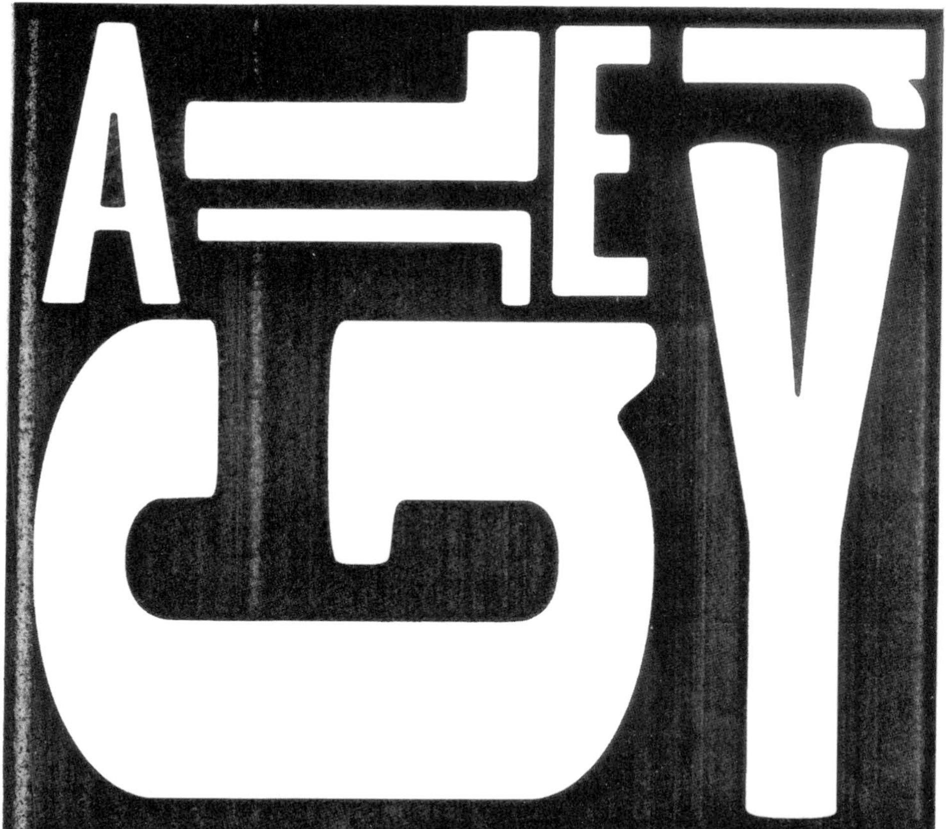

Audio A's Bob Herdman, with wife Jeanette and son Waylen.

Years before Audio A, Bob served his country as an Army Ranger.

Audio Adrenaline concerts are packed with all of the energy and power one would expect from a leading rock and roll performance.

Tyler, most definitely going up.

ABOVE: Ben Cissell, taking a siesta with his childhood pal, Cookie Monster. RIGHT: Christmas at the Cissell house, complete with some pretty spiffy jammies.

BELOW: Ben, displaying the winsome smile that would one day make nightly appearances in Audio A concerts. RIGHT: Animal, eat your heart out!

*Audio Adrenaline's Mark Stuart is one of the most
compelling lead singers in rock music.*

In concert, Mark Stuart commands the attention of his audience like no one else.

Mark, reaching out to his fans both figuratively and literally.

ABOVE: Ride'em cowboy! RIGHT: Tyler, lakeside. His incredible musicianship has quickly made him a world-renowned guitarist.

LEFT: Tyler and wife Alison. BELOW: From Omaha to Nashville, Tyler's presence in Audio A is both unmistakable and irreplaceable.

Audio A bassist Will McGinniss is always a crowd favorite.

After growing up in Ohio, and attending college in Kentucky, Will now travels the world to share his faith in Jesus.

The Distance, Petra, and maybe one early dcTalk show.

"[What] I loved so much was just the fact that they had a message that was really powerful. That inspired me. The fact that they could be so bold about something and be

ONE ON ONE

Will McGinniss is the core of Audio Adrenaline...the heart and soul." —Mark Stuart

"Bill has a very cool heart. He's one of those friends you know would do anything for you. But at the same time, he'll, like, borrow your shoes and you're like, 'What the heck?' He's a very giving person...a really cool guy." —Tyler Burkum

"Will has got the best heart of anybody for kids and likes to reach out to kids the most. Just about every night I pull a prank on Will. I just get the biggest bucket of cold water I can find and dump it on him in the shower. They know I'm gonna do it every night, and every night I somehow surprise him." —Ben Cissell

in a rock band and actually do it full time—that was just really cool to me."

That boldness was a characteristic that Will claimed for himself. Today, he continues to confidently share his testimony to audiences worldwide. He also shared his faith much closer to home.

"Will has a lot of tenacity," says Mark. "I've watched him bury both of his parents. He's been

Beware of the flying hair: an exuberant Will lets loose during an Audio Adrenaline show.

through so much. He came out of a non-Christian family. He has the greatest testimony you could ever listen to. He was saved out of his family. He went back, got his sister saved, then his other sister, then his mom before she died of cancer and then his dad before he died of cancer. So Bill is kind of my hero. I love him to death."

The boy who once felt "unloved" is today a man who's loved by many: audiences, his fellow bandmates, and his family, particularly his wife, Andrea, and little boy, Satchel. Yet, despite widespread acceptance, Will today still feels like a

Wide-eyed Satchel McGinniss: Audio A's littlest fan.

rebel. Only now, he's a rebel *with* a cause.

"I think Jesus is the most rebellious person that ever walked the face of the earth," he says, "and I have kind of a rebellious nature—mostly in a bad way when I was growing up. As of late, I've wanted to be rebellious in going against the norm and really rebellious [for] Christ. He's number one."

When asked about his dreams, Will maintains that his greatest goal in life is simply to serve the God who brought him healing and wholeness.

Whatever the future holds, he says, "I know I'll [always] be doing something [for him]."

Bob Herdman, the man who caught the vision
for Audio Adrenaline.

BOB HERDMAN DIDN'T HAVE AN IOTA OF MUSICAL EXPERIENCE

when he first caught the vision for Audio Adrenaline.

But he did have a way with words.

"I used to write weird poems in the army once in a

while, just to goof off—just to be stupid," he says. But

Bob's gift for verse became even more evident during his

AUDIO Q&A:

The Greatest Challenges of Being in a Band, According to Bob: "I think, for any band, it's a challenge to go through the lean years and be focused on what you want to do—even though your peers have graduated from college and have jobs and get paid good and are starting families. Then here you are: you're still living with your college buddies in a two-room apartment, driving around in an old junky van, wearing long hair, and you kind of feel like a disgrace sometimes. You have to get through those times. That's always a challenge. You don't really think too much about it because you're having a good time. But there are times you think, 'Maybe I should grow up and get a real job.'" —Bob Herdman

Q: Where was Bob during Underdog?
A: Fans who noticed something missing on Audio Adrenaline's Underdog tour needn't fear. Bob Herdman wasn't present in body (although he did appear via video at some venues, singing "The Houseplant Song"), yet he is still a vitally important member of Audio Adrenaline. During the start-up phase of FlickerRecords.com, however—the new label launched by partners Mark Stuart, Will McGinniss, and Bob Herdman—Bob stayed home to run the show. For the time being, says Will, Bob "decided it was more important for him to run the label than for him to play guitar. Just for this season, it was more important for him to get that started."

college years, following his stint in the armed forces.

"In American Literature we had to read all these stories and poems," he explains. "I thought they were horrible. I just didn't get it. I don't know if I'm dumb or what. Barry and I were in that class together and I said, 'I could write stuff like this.'

"So we would just sit at the computer and type out words that rhymed and I'd stick them on the wall outside my dorm room. People would come by, and they would be reading it and trying to analyze it—and we'd just made it up off the top of our heads! So it really kind of started as a joke, but then I guess I maybe had a little bit of a flair—although, you know, a lot of people would say I didn't," he laughs. "We had a lot of bad critiques!"

"He wrote under [the name] C. E. Hobenogen," remembers Will. "On boards, wherever he could find, he would write the most bizarre poems you ever read in your life. That was just the kind of guy he was. If he was bored, he'd just find something to do—a practical joke to everything."

Before long, however, Bob's offbeat writings would bear real fruit. He first wrote the lyrics to "DC-10," a quirky little song about death and the afterlife that was recorded by A-180. Later, "DC-10" appeared on Audio Adrenaline's self-titled debut with ForeFront, and again as a rockabilly version on *Underdog*.

"Most of the stuff I wrote was funny, tongue-in-cheek," he says. "Over the last ten years, [I've been] trying to be a little more serious and be a better writer. But I don't take it too seriously."

While growing up in the little town of Lynchburg, Ohio, reaching out to the world with the gospel—through song or otherwise—was the last thing on Bob's mind. Though he had become saved at the age of nine, Bob says: "In some ways I just took it for granted. I've pretty much had the knowledge in my life, my whole life. I grew up going to church, became a

Christian. [But] I wasn't really that strong. I didn't drink, smoke, cuss, or do anything—but there's more to Christianity than that, of course.

"Then I joined the army and went through four years of rebellion. I knew it was wrong. So I got out of the army and thought, I'll go to Bible college for a year and get straightened up."

Bob did, indeed, get "straightened up," though he maintained the creativity and intensity that had been his throughout his late teens and early twenties. Those traits came in handy as he slipped into his new role in Audio Adrenaline.

"When we first started [the group], I wasn't really going to be in it," he remembers. "Then we moved [to Nashville]. I don't know what I was going to do: write lyrics, manage,

ONE ON ONE

"**Bob's the spark plug to Audio Adrenaline.** [What] he lacks in musical ability he makes up for in his sense of grandeur. He's a big picture guy, very bold. Bob is kind of the ignitor of the whole thing." —Mark Stuart

"**Bob's been the guy that** [says], 'You know what? Focus on this. We need to keep youth pastors in mind when we do this. We need to remember what the kids want.'" —Will McGinniss

"**Bob is very wacky.** He cannot be pigeonholed. He's just so crazy...he's weird. He can go from being like the life of the party to intense—driving everybody crazy. He's controversial, and he would love to hear me say that. He would laugh hard if I said that. He probably wants to be controversial." —Tyler Burkum

"**I'm just scared of him.** He's nuts. That's the truth. He was an Army Ranger and I think anytime he's just going to snap. I don't know what I can say about him. I never really have done any practical jokes to him because I'm afraid he's going to kill me." —Ben Cissell

or something else. For some reason we decided I should be in it." Once again, Barry Blair took on the role of music teacher. "I didn't have any musical skills at all. Barry was a great musician. Basically he taught me these chords on a keyboard. Like a rote monkey, I would hold these fingers down and then count to four, and hold these fingers down and count to eight, and hold these notes down....I did that for a couple years and I really didn't like it. I just did it because I did it. Then I kind of started playing the guitar on my own and learning." Eventually, Bob moved into playing rhythm guitar full-time.

Few people would charge into foreign territory so willingly. Yet for Bob, accepting the challenges came naturally.

"Bob's a risk-taker," Mark explains. "Someone who likes to shake things up and do stuff different."

That's not to say that there haven't been challenges. Though his dream of being in a band was fully realized, Bob is the first to admit that the demands of life in a band have at times been difficult—despite the support of his wife, Jeanette, lead singer of Considering Lily, and his young son, Waylen, and new daughter, Parker. He's also the first to say the eternal rewards have been worth the personal sacrifice.

"There's one [song] on *Some Kind of Zombie* called 'Flicker.' It's basically about doing what we do. *My old friends, haven't seen them since I don't know when / but I can send them a signed 8 by 10 / My sweetheart, she understands why I'm away / but still it gets harder every day.* Being on the road, being gone a lot—you don't have time to see all your old college buddies. They want to hang out; you just don't have time anymore. You're gone from your family a lot but your wife understands that you're doing a ministry. There's different lines like that in the song. But the chorus says: *But it's my delight to sing all night...just to share a flicker of God's hope.*

"I think that has to do with us as a band. There's a lot of great stuff that happens to you, but there are sacrifices. We're doing this to share just a little bit of God's light and love to kids out there."

"We're not the best song writers. We're definitely not the best looking." The bottom line reason for their success? "God's hand has been in it," Bob says.

"If God chooses you, you could have really no strengths and you're going to make it."

Ben Cissell's note to self: Never spar with Evander Holyfield.

WHEN ASKED WHO HAS INSPIRED HIM MUSICALLY,

the average drummer might list legends like

John Bonham from Led Zepplin or Stuart

Copeland of The Police, or one of many

jazz heroes. Few would admit to being

shaped, artistically, by a puppet.

AUDIO Q&A:

Ben's Pet Miracle

"I have a dog that lives with my parents. I got him on my eighth birthday, but since I'm gone so much I can't take care of him. His name is Pelé. He's a little toy poodle, about 15-16 inches. The vets can't believe it because about four years ago—and now about every six months—[they keep saying.] this should be his last week. But he just keeps living."

Ben's Current Obsession

"Ben's into anything that has to do with creativity. Especially with the visual. Right now he's into videos. That's all he does is take videos and sit at the back of the bus and edit together videos. Ben is one of the biggest advocates for Audio Adrenaline as it comes to big ideas and cool concepts." —Mark Stuart

Ben's Pet Musical Peeve

"My senior year [in high school], I couldn't play soccer or football, and I joined the marching band and I hated that. A marching band represents everything that I'm against in music. I think music should be a sense of freedom and expression. A marching band is like discipline and that's it. You have to be right here and you have to be on this note and don't stray from it. So I never really got marching bands." —Ben Cissell

Ben Cissell is not the average drummer.

"I was a hyperactive kid and I liked the Muppets. Still today, Animal is one of my biggest drum influences," he says seriously. "I got a Muppets drum set when I was probably four. Then my dad bought me a real drum set when I was in fourth grade, but I didn't really get serious about playing drums until about eighth or ninth grade when I started this little punk band, Donut."

Born in Richardson, Texas, Ben also lived in Oklahoma and Missouri while growing up, but it was in St. Louis—where he lived from fifth grade through his freshman year of college—that his musical career began. Along with Donut, Ben played in a band called Stone Forest—and later, the funk band Funkopotomus.

"I also played drums for praise and worship for this church. My parents used to think it was so funny because [I had] Thursday night jazz recital, Friday night I would be playing downtown in some smoky bar with Donut, Saturday night I would be doing the same thing with Stone Forest, then Sunday morning I would wake up really early

BEN'S MOST EMBARRASSING MOMENT

"My parents let me borrow their camcorder when I was on the Steven Curtis Chapman tour and I brought my first videotape home to show them and I hadn't watched it yet. I wanted to show them what I did. They didn't really understand; they thought I dropped out of college and joined the circus.

"So I brought this tape home and it was Thanksgiving. Both sets of grandparents, aunt and uncle, brother and sister were down in the basement watching this. And one of our crew guys, without me knowing it, [had taken] the camera and filmed one of the guys in the shower for about 3 seconds. So I'm just watching—it's all nice and everything—and all of a sudden—bleep—it's a naked band member. So my parents are always making fun of me for that.

"I haven't told any of the band members that though."

and go play praise and worship. It was pretty neat because I got to meet a lot of

different people."

Although he became a Christian at a Young Life camp during his sophomore year

of high school, Ben never was drawn to Christian music as a teen.

He remembers the time in the eighth grade when his friend Chris Connelly tried to play him a tape by a popular Christian music group. "I said, 'That's awful, Chris. What are you listening to?'"

Then, during Ben's senior year in high school, Chris and another friend invited him to go with them to a Newsboys/Audio Adrenaline concert. "I made fun of them," he admits. "I went, 'a Christian rock tour?' Chris and this guy Phil Hunter really wanted me to see this band called Audio Adrenaline. They thought I'd really like

Cissell gives it all he's got during an Audio A performance.

ONE ON ONE

"**Ben adds a lot of a sense of humor** to Audio Adrenaline and a lot of the fun. Where I might be a little too serious and Tyler might be a little too musically into this, Ben will bring it back to reality because he realizes that we're just up there playing music and it's not the end of the world if something goes wrong. He always plays with a smile. Ben's core of the comedy." —Mark Stuart

"**Ben is super creative. He's a prankster**—a practical joke guy. He loves being the center of the fun. If it's boring out here, it's his duty to liven it up. He's Mr. Gadget, too. He's very good with making anything he might need. He built his own underwater camera case for his video camera out of an old army artillery case. He's definitely very MacGyverish." —Will McGinniss

"**Ben is very boyish,** not like a little boy, but he can go from just being a normal twenty-five-year-old guy, then be pulling a practical joke like a little kid. It is more of a spirit thing. He can be the encouraging guy and he can be the angry-rebellious guy. He's basically what everybody is not at that time. So if all of us are serious, he's pulling practical jokes. If all of us are calm, he's like: 'We've got to do something!'" —Tyler Burkum

"**Ben is fun-loving, easy-going, joyful.** He likes to goof off a lot. He's kind of a big kid, really. He has been a huge kid. He's a very outgoing person. People love Ben and he can talk to anybody." —Bob Herdman

them. They actually bought me a ticket and I refused, and they had to end up giving the ticket away."

That tour was *Going Public*. Ironically, Ben was on the next tour that Audio Adrenaline played: dcTalk's 1996 *Jesus Freak* tour—the biggest Christian music tour of its time.

But Ben's introduction to the band, surprisingly, was not as a drummer.

"I had dropped out of college, and my mom and dad weren't very happy with me," he recalls. "And I had a friend, Jeff, who was in a band called East to West. He said, 'Why don't you come down to Nashville for a while and sell T-shirts for us?' So I moved to Nashville not knowing why, not knowing anything about Christian music."

Because Jeff was best friends with Scott Brickell, Audio Adrenaline's manager, that move ultimately led to a job selling T-shirts for Audio A. While serving in this role, Ben noticed that Mark, Will, and Bob were watching drum audition tapes.

He thought to himself: *I'm a drummer.*

"But instead of really saying that and offering it right away," he says, "I quietly watched all the drum audition videos. They knew I was a drummer, but they just thought I played around. So the whole time I'm working with them, for six months, I'm watching all these drum audition videos and listening…and by the time my audition comes up, I know exactly what kind of drummer they want by watching all these videos. So I kind of stole the gig from everybody else that auditioned." He grins. "And I don't feel bad about it."

Another thing Ben doesn't feel bad about is the infamous practical jokes he plays on his bandmates.

"Mostly it is me that he gets," sighs Will.

When the other members of Audio Adrenaline are out of the room, Ben grins smugly. "On April Fool's Day, I'm about to get all the guys really bad. I'm going to put Sprite in all their water bottles so when they go to take a big swig of water, they're just

Field of dreams: Ben's early years, before he sold T-shirts for the band and eventually became the drummer.

going to get spray. You know what a big shock that is? On stage, you only have about five seconds to drink water and you usually just slam it." He smirks. "So it will be a good shock."

When asked what he thought he'd be when he grew up, he confesses: "I never thought I'd grow up. I haven't grown up. I don't know. I've always been one of those people who's kind of happy where I'm at. I can always make the best of what's going on, so I never really cared."

If there's one thing Ben does care about, passionately, it's the impact Audio Adrenaline has on its audience.

"If I didn't feel like I was making a difference or edifying or evangelizing to somebody, I would be fine doing a landscaping company, mowing yards or doing whatever. Because I could be at home spending time really working on stuff—but this is what I am called to do. [Sometimes you wonder]: 'What's going on? Why am I out here?' Right when you start to question if what you're doing is really a ministry or is this doing anything for the kingdom—that's when God sends somebody or you talk to somebody [who's been touched] and that puts you right back on track. Those times come at the best time."

Tyler Burkum, the latest addition to Audio Adrenaline.

JOINING A SUCCESSFUL ROCK GROUP is the nearly universal dream of budding 17-year-old musicians. But for Tyler Burkum, the transition from high school student to lead guitarist was as natural as breathing.

"My dad is a musician and I played with him," says Tyler. "I grew up singing with him and playing at home, church or anywhere. It was kind of weird because I did music my whole life, growing up, so I felt like it was ingrained into me."

Though his training was solid, his experience was fairly limited. "I really hadn't done that much. I was just kind of playing with friends in a couple local bands. I was in a band called Snappy, then a band called 9-Acre Smile. My time with both was very short. I just kind of played around with everybody." From such local experience, Tyler moved easily into his role with Audio Adrenaline. "For being such a big change, jumping into music full-time, it was kind of weird how natural that was."

That smooth transition can be attributed, at least in part, to Tyler's inherent talent.

Another key factor was the value placed on music by his family, including his grandfather, a college music professor, and his father and uncle, both musicians.

From this family legacy, Tyler learned early in life to approach music not as a hobby, but as a lifestyle. During his high school years, he was homeschooled so that he could play at local venues in the evenings without causing his studies to suffer. He was, in fact, still in school—though near the end of his final year—when he learned about

"I am sooooo strong...:" Tyler clowns for a publicity shot for the band's Underdog project.

AUDIO Q&A

Q: What was the birthplace of Audio Adrenaline's lead guitarist?
A: Tyler Burkum was born in Lincoln, Nebraska, on December 31, 1979. (It's "My Three Sons" for the Burkums. Tyler is the eldest child in his family, with two younger brothers: Page and Torrey.)

Q: How did Tyler get his start musically?
A: "I didn't start playing guitar until I was like seven or eight, but I was raised my whole life singing. My grandparents sang and every dinnertime was a singing event; we would sing the Doxology. I sang 'Amen' about 3 times a day."
—Tyler Burkum

Tyler's European Vacation
"[When we were in Europe], some train in Italy broke down. I was on my way to the airport in Rome and I was just trying to fly to a show in Sweden. So I missed the last flight. Instead of flying to Munich, I had to fly to Frankfurt, sleep on the airport floor. All this time I was supposed to be there the night before, but I didn't think it was that big of a deal. I was thinking, okay I'll just be there the morning of. I didn't have any money on me or anything, and I didn't know the country code. So I get there and they are just furious because they thought I was lost in Europe, something dumb like that. They'd already hired another guitar player from another band, teaching him the songs and everything, thinking I wasn't going to be there. It was just hilarious. They were so mad at me." —Tyler Burkum

the opening with Audio Adrenaline from an acquaintance who had moved to Nashville.

A series of auditions followed: first by videotape, then in Minnesota when Audio Adrenaline swept through town.

"About a month and a

half later I auditioned again in Nashville," says Tyler. "Then two months went by and I got a phone call." The band was not yet ready to bring him on full-time, but they did want him to come on board for a trial run—starting in two weeks.

The rest is Christian music history.

Just a few years after leaving his parents' home, Tyler now leads a vastly different life than he did as a teen. Today, he's not only the much-admired lead guitarist of one of Christian music's top bands, he's also a loving husband to his wife Alison. And though Tyler has been in Audio Adrenaline just a few years, it feels to him almost as though he's been with them from the beginning.

"There are things that I wasn't around for that I've heard about so many times, I can tell the stories like I was there—because I've heard these guys tell every angle of it. It feels very natural for me to be in this band. It feels like I've been here all along. I don't know how it feels for them, but that's how it feels for me."

One thing the other band members feel is amazed by his abilities.

"Musically, he's brilliant," says Mark. "Even lyrically, he's brilliant. He

OK, which one's Tyler? (Hint: He's not wearing a tie.)

has tons of unharnessed musical and artistic talent."

Will agrees. "Not a day goes by that he doesn't cease to amaze me with his raw talent, his complete and utterly amazing gift from God."

Tyler remains philosophical—and humble.

"I'm not a prodigy or anything. There are plenty of things that are just hard for anybody. But some aspects of music are as natural as breathing. Probably the only thing that's as natural in my life is love. I can barely walk...I'm a klutz...I fall all the time. I never wanted to be some star or anything, and I don't think I am. I was never as intentional as that. I'm just kind of along for the ride."

And he's not wasting a single minute of it.

ONE ON ONE

"Tyler is the musician in the band." —Bob Herdman

"Tyler is like a breath of fresh air with a twist. I feel somewhat like his big brother on his musical journey. I'm trying not to get in his way at all, because he's way more talented than I am. He's like the Tasmanian devil: he has some quirks about his personality that are just nuts. He's like my little brother and I love him dearly." —Mark Stuart

"Tyler is the typical guitar player in the fact that he's the most talented guy in the band, probably. For his age, he's just a prodigy. He catches a lot of the brunt of the pranks because he's the youngest and I don't think that's quite fair—but I guess that happens. He can take it." —Will McGinniss

"Tyler is the stereotype of every guitar player. He'll (do sound) check for an hour. I've de-tuned his guitar, taken off his strap. I unplug his amp..." —Ben Cissell

"I would like to get better. I really beat myself up when I do stupid things—not just in music, but in life. I don't want to waste experiences that will make me a better musician or a better person. One of the hardest things to realize is that if you know there's a God and you're living for him, that's all you can do—so don't stress out about the little things.

"For the most part, I really love this job. You know, you get to travel everywhere. That's a really cool thing. But it comes down to relationships. It's really very cool to be in a band with people you can trust and you really love and can be brothers with."

The adrenaline is flowing: capturing the energy of an Audio A show.

IN SPITE OF THE PHENOMENAL SUCCESS Audio Adrenaline has achieved in the Christian music industry, the guys in the band wave off any suggestions of brilliance, suggesting another reason for their popularity with audiences.

"Probably [it's] because we're just regular guys," reasons Will. "We love to snow-board and we're really just college boys. Musically, we don't really take ourselves very seriously. We try to play good music. But music is not the end all for us. We just try to be joyful."

> "Musically, we don't really take ourselves very seriously. We try to play good music. But music is not the end all for us. We just try to be joyful."

Unconcerned with maintaining a polished, professional image, the guys eagerly offer accounts of the ego-busting experiences they've shared as a band—most of which have involved their fearless frontman.

"We tape 'kick me' signs on the back of Mark all the time," says Tyler. "Like, we give him a little pat or a little hug before we go on stage and he's like, 'Do I look cool?' And we're like, 'Yeah, you look great.' And he walks out there and then our monitor guy tells him in his ear, in the middle of the show, 'Do you really want me to kick you?'"

Mark particularly remembers one disastrous event. "On the Geoff Moore tour, I was backstage and we were getting ready to go on. I was all ready to go, I had my outfit on, and I hear them saying 'Audio Adrenaline will be right out.' Then I'm walking towards what I thought was the stage and I fell—behind the stage, up to my waist— into the baptistery, which happened to be right in the back of the background. I could see the crowd and everybody looking around for me. I had to wait and stop the show for a few minutes until I changed clothes."

Ben has his own favorite story about Audio A's lead singer. "Mark has forgotten what city we are in a lot, but

Let the sunshine in: Audio A takes a break from rehearsals.

he's so witty. One time, he got up there and we were in Augusta, Georgia, and he thought we were in Atlanta, and he goes: 'What's up, Atlanta?' and everybody goes, 'Augusta!' And he goes, 'Oh, yeah. I thought this place was cool.' So that was a good recovery."

Another time, while on the Steven Curtis Chapman

> Ben says that he hopes that in the future, "when Audio Adrenaline is done, people can just say, 'that was real.'"

tour, Mark went snowblind while skiing in the Arapaho basin.

"They had to put patches on his eyes," recalls Bob, "so he had these sunglasses on and someone had to lead him onstage. If you didn't know what was going on, it just looked like, *What a prima donna*. He walked out there with these sunglasses on; he was holding on to his microphone and not moving. But he really was blind that night."

None of the band members—not even Mark—mind if they are remembered for real moments like these.

Ben says that he hopes that in the future, "when Audio Adrenaline is done, people can just say, 'That was real. What you guys did was real. It wasn't an act or a show.'"

Mark agrees that the point is not to impress the masses.

"If we're talking about respect from men, I would much rather be looked upon favorably by our peers and people that we have worked with—people that are in the band, the crew, our record company. [I want them to be able] to say that we were real like that. God can pick another band to get up here and do what we do. He's more concerned about our everyday lives and how we treat people—and how we love each other—than how many Dove Awards [we win] or how many songs we can get to number one on the charts."

The guitar waits...as the band rocks.

WITH A NEW MILLENNIUM COMES NEW CHALLENGES—and

Audio Adrenaline is enjoying each opportunity that

comes their way.

Fans can look for that future to include more

production gigs for Mark Stuart, who produced

Jennifer Knapp's *Kansas* and *Lay It Down*, and

more songwriting for Bob Herdman, who has also contributed to albums by Bleach and Considering Lily. Undoubtedly, Ben Cissell, Will McGinniss, and Tyler Burkum (who also played on *Kansas* and *Lay It Down*) will all continue to develop their considerable talent as musicians.

As the Audio Adrenaline "family" keeps on growing (Will and Bob have already begun adding children to the mix), additional adjustments will almost certainly need to be made. But the band members give every indication that—challenges or

All together now: The Audio A guys are in tune with their music and each other.

not—they're in this for the long haul.

With this goal in mind, Bob, Mark, and Will recently joined forces to create a new independent label, FlickerRecords.com, to serve talented young artists who share their ministry philosophy—those who, Mark says, he and his partners "feel are creatively legit and musically brilliant, but also have a heart for God."

In 1999, FlickerRecords.com signed its first such artist: Canadian Riley Armstrong, who opened for Audio Adrenaline on the *Underdog* tour. They have also signed Kansas-based rock/rap/core band Pillar.

Do such developments mean that the band's focus is changing?

The answer, says Bob Herdman, is yes…and no.

"We're looking toward the future," he explains. "You know, you can't jump around—and 14-year-old kids are not going to want to see you—forever. We understand that."

"Flicker is a way for us to be involved in Christian music on a different level," Mark counters. "It's a way for us to start building roots."

"There's a lot we believe we've learned over the last 10 years or so," says Bob, "and we want to pass that on to younger bands, and help them, and be involved in the shaping of Christian music in the future."

Fans needn't worry, however, that Flicker Records will distract Audio Adrenaline from making the music they love.

"This [Christian music] is what I want to do for the rest of my life," say Mark. "If it's with Audio Adrenaline, that's great."

"As long as God keeps blessing us with people coming to our shows," Bob vows, "we'll keep doing it. We believe God chose us for this. All these things in our lives have just happened, and I believe it's because of him. We're not the best musicians by far. We're not the best songwriters. We're definitely not the best looking." The bottom line reason for their success? "God's hand has been in it," Bob says.

"If God chooses you, you could have really no strengths and you're going to make it."

Stuart and the band perform for now and look toward the future.